MICHIGAN in a century and a half has built a magnificent tradition of challenging adversity, solving its problems, and ending up with opportunities for new successes. It is a diverse state with dedicated and productive citizens from many backgrounds. Michigan is blessed with the widest spectrum of natural resources, especially the magnificence of Lakes Michigan, Huron, and Superior. Its mineral resources, natural gas deposits, and oil reserves are invaluable assets, and the variety and quality of agricultural production are significant. Michigan is recognized for its superb industrial output, with management and unions working together to meet the challenge of business competition.

History demonstrates that the citizens of Michigan have always insisted on excellence. The future of Michigan is unlimited.

Gerald R. Ford

GERALD R. FORD

To my strongest ties to Michigan: to Monica, Christian, and Alexandra.

My gratitude goes to Gary Quesada for his important contribution to this work.

BALTHAZAR KORAB

Designed by Marilyn F. Appleby and Josef Beery.
Edited by Michael P. Spradlin and Carlotta M. Eike.
Photography copyright ©1987 by Balthazar Korab. All rights reserved.
Introduction copyright ©1987 by William G. Milliken. All rights reserved.
This book, or any portions thereof, may not be reproduced
or transmitted in any form or by any means, electronic or mechanical,
including photocopying, recording, or by any
information storage and retrieval system, without permission in writing from the publisher.
Photography may not be reproduced without permission of Balthazar Korab.
Introduction may not be reproduced without permission of William G. Milliken.
Library of Congress Catalog Card Number 86-82666
ISBN 0-9616878-4-3
Printed and bound in Hong Kong by Everbest Printing Co., Ltd.
for Four Colour Imports, Ltd., Louisville, Kentucky.
Published by Howell Press, Inc., 2000 Holiday Drive,
Charlottesville, Virginia 22901. Telephone (804) 977-4006.
First edition
Spradlin-Patrick is an imprint of Howell Press, Inc.

SPRADLIN-PATRICK

MICHIGAN

PHOTOGRAPHY BY BALTHAZAR KORAB

INTRODUCTION BY WILLIAM G. MILLIKEN

MICHIGAN has never really had a present moment. It has a mysterious past and an incalculable future, attractive and terrifying by turns, but the moment where the two meet is always a time of transition. The state is caught between yesterday and tomorrow, existing less for itself than for what it leads to; it is a road where ends are distorted by imagination and imperfect knowledge. The great American feeling of being en route — to the unknown, to something new, to the fantastic reality that must lie beyond the mists is perfectly represented here.

BRUCE CATTON, *Michigan: A Bicentennial History*, 1976.

A PRESENT MOMENT

ONCE IN A WHILE A PERCEPTION takes hold of reality and becomes more authentic than the truth. So it is with Michigan. Wherever I have traveled outside my home state, the perception of Michigan that greeted me was one of great size, vast industry, and rich congestion. Large, noisy, hustling, turbulent, problem-ridden — these words brought Michigan to mind from Maine to Munich.

Michigan is all of these things, of course, and yet the description remains essentially wrong. Michigan is so much more.

If one's vision of the state is bounded by smoke-stacks, then the Lake Superior shoreline, clenched in the frozen fist of winter, must be some other place. But the glacial solitude of that "other place" is Michigan as surely as sparks that shower from a robot's welding finger. And the contrast helps define this place of unparalleled diversity — of landscape, of resources, of people.

In his remarkable book, *America*, Alistair Cooke confronted a similar dilemma in describing our nation to the British — "nothing you say about the whole country is going to be true."

Held in the embrace of four Great Lakes, Michigan is a land where water has been the unifying force of destiny and will most certainly remain so in the future. In Michigan waters, civilization and wilderness contrast vividly — from the dynamic Detroit riverfront where passing freighters speak the international language of industrial navigation to the sheltered calm of Les Cheneaux Islands adrift at the top of Lake Huron.

It was my privilege for many years to enjoy the view from Michigan's "front porch" — the governor's summer house on Mackinac Island. It overlooks both peninsulas, and from its weathered height the diversity of Michigan unfolds before the eye. Extraordinary splendor stretches into every distance while through the straits below pass the riches of Michigan products en route to unseen horizons. In this single scene, the sharp variety of Michigan life is revealed.

Only the industrial nature of Michigan is widely known, its boom-and-bust cycles chronicled by the national press. Centuries before either press or nation, the initial boom began with a thriving trade in furs between the French and native Indians. The first to be interested in "Michigan products," the French sent two hugely differing types of men here from Montreal: intrepid *voyageurs* who trapped, traded, and explored the primal wilderness and Jesuit priests (explorers by inclination if not by trade) who taught and preached among the Indians.

Shortly after came French soldiers to protect the investment in pelts and souls. The French remain today in the names of Michigan towns: St. Ignace, Sault Ste. Marie, Marquette, Detroit. So great was the value of Michigan furs that the English and French battled frequently to control it, and the United States was hardly established before joining the fight for a share of the riches. The final losers in all engagements were the Indians, left with little more than another legacy of place-names: Mackinac, Tecumseh, Kalamazoo, Ottawa, Michigan.

John Jacob Astor was the biggest winner in Michigan's fur trade, but other fortunes were made as well, and a significant pattern was set: judge the wealth of a resource, work against great odds to use it, abandon it at exhaustion. The pattern was repeated with copper, iron ore, and lumber. Vast fortunes were made, thousands of men endured incredible labor harvesting the wealth, and then the resource was gone.

The "gobble and go" theory of settlement, in spite of its manifest faults, had a positive side. It expressed in exuberant excess the essentially American spirit of great expectations based on seemingly unlimited resources and equally unlimited ingenuity. First with fur, again with lumber, yet again with copper and iron ore, and to a degree, even with cities, the past was casually discarded in favor of a more promising future — a future made possible and even inevitable by abundance in natural wealth. In fact, abundance has fueled the history of Michigan and shaped its character, a point made best by Pulitzer Prize-winning historian and Michigan native, Bruce Catton — "inexhaustible — that fatal Michigan word."

As a result, boom-and-bust has been a leitmotif of Michigan history from the lucrative fur trade to the enormous prosperity and wrenching dislocations of the auto industry.

The highs were very high indeed. Millions and millions of board feet of lumber were turned out from the white pine stands of the Saginaw Valley alone, and the state's west side produced millions more. One estimate put its value in the last half of the 19th century at con-

siderably more than California's gold in the same period. In addition to the direct work and wealth, this production spawned a thriving furniture industry and promoted vastly increased settlement throughout Michigan. In the natural course of things, the lumber nearest the rivers was cut first and floated to the mills after the spring thaw. As river-accessible trees were felled, different transportation was needed, and the impetus was born for a far-flung expansion of railroads into previously impenetrable areas of the state.

Transportation also governed the mining of copper and iron ore. Its presence in untold quantity and quality had long been known, but not until the building of the Soo Locks could the richest lodes yet discovered in the country be profitably brought to market.

The settlers, the farming people, came rather late to Michigan, put off in part by the first instance of what was later known as "bad press." Earliest reports from the area informed land-hungry easterners that Michigan was a swamp of endless dimensions unfit for man or beast. What's more, fever was said to abound from the hordes of insects, and the place was, in general, a "land of ills." Once again transportation took a hand in Michigan's history. With the opening of the Erie Canal, a flood of settlers saw for themselves that the southern lower peninsula was a lush and fertile garden — or at least it could be both with the hard work of determined farmers. In its turn, the canal gave access to eastern markets for the products of these ambitious pioneers.

These are the people who came to stay, to build lives rather than fortunes. Nearly two centuries earlier, Antoine Cadillac had tried to persuade the French to do just that. He brought his wife — the only serious indication that a new land is to be home. Had he been more persuasive, our state might have flown the French flag for many more generations.

The grinding labor of resolute pioneers brought forth a thriving harmony with the land of southern Michigan — still more abundance. Of equal importance, it gave rise to the creation of communities which in turn attracted more settlers and formed the foundation for Michigan's future.

Unhappily, the labor of some settlers produced no more than a crop of stumps and disappointments. As land was opened by the lumber harvest, thousands of would-be farmers trekked north. But the towering pines of the northern lower peninsula sheltered soil unlike the fertile acres of the south. Occasionally in rural Michigan today, the silent witness of those lost hopes endures — an abandoned farmhouse with hollow-eyed windows, doors that sag like discouraged shoulders, and no whisper of the promise that must have shaped the house so long ago.

Such disillusion was an exception to the rule of plenty. Michigan agriculture today attests to the foresight and perseverance of the early settlers: from first to fifth among the states in the production of about 20 foods, adding nearly $20 billion to the economy.

The wealth, the industry, the family factories and businesses, the farms, and most of all, the people drawn to Michigan originally for its rich resources, furnished all the elements needed for Michigan to roll headlong into the 20th century on wheels. The people came from nearly every corner of the globe, and they turned out to be the richest resources of all — the brains and brawn that powered the industrial age.

The French came to trade; the Cornish to mine; the Finns, other Scandinavians, French Canadians, and Maine Yankees to hew the state out of the wilderness; the Dutch to settle west Michigan's farms still thriving today; the Irish to build railroads; Germans and Italians to establish small factories and shops; and a multitude of Poles and eastern Europeans to propel assembly lines. Thousands of blacks and southern whites came to find a piece of plenty in exchange for their labor.

Like everyone before them, the immigrants took to the belief in boundless possibility (a natural credo for immigrants) which needed only a place for tomorrow to happen. The history of how it happened here is the Michigan known around the world...of production lines paying $5 a day...of a vast new market of Everyman made mobile... of war production churning out planes and tanks in numbers beyond all probability...of prosperity that invited laborers to become homeowners...of college degrees for sons and daughters of the factory...of working men and women who discovered for the first time the power of their labor.

The names of those who shaped Michigan's history are far too numerous to mention. A few ring with acclaim — Henry Ford, Antoine Cadillac, George Rogers Clark, Père Marquette, Walter Reuther. Others wielded great influence in their time but faded from renown — Lewis Cass, Chief Pontiac, Stevens Mason, Laura Smith Haviland.

Among them was Chase Osborn, governor of Michigan in the early years of this century. Under his progressive direction, Michigan initiated a workmen's compensation law, made many efforts toward voting reform, ran a surplus budget, and at long last took an interest in conservation. Osborn was an early supporter of women's suffrage and a man who believed public service was an honorable trade. Many years later, after leaving public service, he took the time to correspond regularly with a teenage boy in Traverse City. He passed on to me his thoughts about public service, his abiding love of Michigan, and — wonderfully — one dollar with each letter. As befitted a native of the north country, Governor Osborn was staunchly individual, yet his belief in working for the general good offered a fine example for young dreams.

Many decades passed before conservation caught the public imagination, but when it came, environmental interest took a very firm hold. I have often said that Michigan has more to gain and more to lose in the handling of land and water than any other place. Perhaps it is fitting that a state which once abused her natural resources to exhaustion now protects those riches with a certain fierceness.

As a result, visitors by the millions enjoy Michigan's four Great Lakes — each with its individual lure familiar to Michiganians. (The weighty question of what to call people from Michigan has occupied many a debate from barroom to legislature. The awkward mouthful "Michiganian" generally wins out over the even less elegant "Michigander.")

It is hard to speak of the largest collection of surface fresh water in the world without lapsing into hyperbole.

By reason of birth, I am partial to the Grand Traverse Bay area of northwestern Michigan. Growing up along its shoreline, I left for school, for war, for work, but I've returned whenever possible for renewal. As a friend tells me, I've always had one foot in the sand. Here Nature has fashioned a special place of wonderful serenity called the Mission Peninsula — a narrow spit of land that thrusts out into the bay and ends at Old Mission. This is home to me — home, as Oliver Wendell Holmes said, "that our feet may leave but not our hearts."

My grandfather came to this part of Michigan in his late teens with a friend of the same age. The talk of new opportunities in the west drew them from their native Maine to Chicago where they heard of even greater promise in a place called Traverse City. They crossed Lake Michigan and arrived in Grand Traverse Bay as dark was falling one Saturday night in 1873. On Sunday morning they rowed ashore and landed at what is now Clinch Park.

Setting off to explore the wonders of their new home, they sank into the wallow of mudholes that served as Traverse City's main street. Here and there a wooden plank fought to stay on top of the mire, but for the most part, mud prevailed. A brief walk through the raw settlement was enough. They returned to the boat where my grandfather recorded the impact of the visit in his diary (I have it still) — "And so we saw Traverse City, Michigan. The less said about it, the better."

But the early settlers were not fainthearted sorts. My grandfather stayed on in spite of the mud, working in a mercantile business until he was able to establish his own retail store. And of course he came to regard Traverse City in a more favorable light than his first impression. It is an area of exquisite natural beauty, clothed in a medley of colors by season, and bordered always in blue.

Much of the Lake Michigan shoreline is lined with high bluffs which further south soften to vast expanses of white sand dunes lightly strewn with sedge grass. Across the state on Lake Huron, the scene is smaller in scale but not in charm, with gentle hills near the Harrisville shore and pebbled beaches further south. More southerly yet, the waters of Lake St. Clair shelter the great muskellunge, its fishermen finding here one of the world's finest breeding grounds for their favorite fish. Also bordering Michigan is the shallower Lake Erie whose obituary was firmly written years ago. Today the lake abounds with walleye and sailors who enjoy its recovered health.

Hundreds of miles away but in the same water system, the Lake Superior shoreline expresses the essence of solitude. This mighty inland sea harbors islands and shores of unspoiled wilderness and hides countless wrecks in its unforgiving depths. From the earliest days, the Upper Peninsula has been a hard land that breeds a hardy people well suited to the trials and triumphs of Superior.

Although a longer coastline than any state except Alaska surrounds Michigan, in an embarrassment of riches, it also boasts more than 11,000 inland lakes and hundreds of rivers and streams. Like the Great Lakes, these waters offer boating, fishing, swimming, camping—a resource for unparalleled vacationing. The extensive state park system makes all the wonders of Michigan available to any who choose to enjoy them.

Within a few miles of Detroit's big-city attractions, a visitor can savor the pleasures of peaceful, rural countryside. Dozens of small towns retain the flavor of an earlier time—here a courthouse draped in wonderful Victorian excess, there a farmhouse turning a face of unadorned utility to the world. Some towns are folded in gently rolling hills and others are separated by miles of flat fertility.

Such variety blesses this state that it's difficult to say whether Michigan is a summer evening among the cheering crowds at Tiger Stadium or a nostalgic carriage ride on Mackinac Island. A Present Moment here is the precision of an automated manufacturing plant, it's the beat of a Motown song, it's the swish of cross-country skis in a hushed forest. As we mark 150 years of statehood, we rejoice in the energetic diversity that is Michigan today.

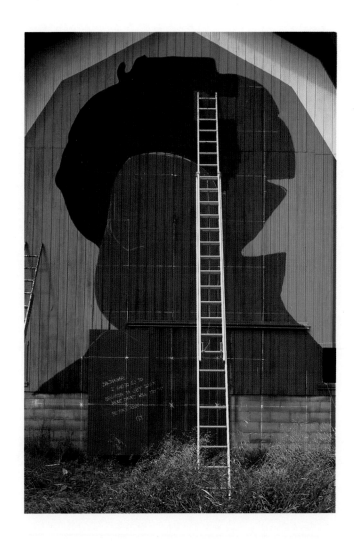

Our past, present, and future moments are inevitably wedded to water — water for industry, agriculture, navigation, domestic, and recreational needs. Water forms another marriage of Michigan to abundance, but we expect to shelter this union safely from our belief in boundless supply.

A lake, Henry David Thoreau said, "is the earth's eye: looking into which the beholder measures the depth of his own nature." Through the eye of Balthazar Korab, this book beholds, measures, and celebrates the splendor that is Michigan and captures the stewards of its heritage in the present moment.

WILLIAM G. MILLIKEN

THE U.P. IS WILD harsh and broken land, rubbed and ground on the relentless hone of many past glaciers, the last one, in its slow convulsive retreat, leaving the country a jumble of swamp and hills and rocks and endless waterways. Lying as it does within the southernmost rim of the great Canadian Pre-Cambrian shield, the region is perhaps more nearly allied with Canada by climatic and geographical affinity; with Wisconsin by the logic of geography; but a region which by some logic beyond logic, finally wound up as part of the state of Michigan; this after a series of political blunders and compromises that doubtless made the angels weep. Nobody had wanted to adopt the remote and raffish U.P. and Michigan was at last persuaded to take it reluctantly, coveting instead, almost to the brink of civil war, a modest parcel of land along the Ohio border known as the "Toledo Strip." This wry political fairy tale unfolded in all of its lovely irony when large copper and iron deposits were shortly discovered on the U.P., rivaling any then known in the hemisphere. The unwanted ugly duckling had turned into a fabulous golden-haired princess.

ROBERT TRAVER, *Anatomy of a Murder,* 1958.

AFTER THE DISCOVERY of a lode or vein — a difficult matter in itself — preparations were at once made to work it, or in other words to open the mine. The first preliminary operation was to make a clearing large enough to make room for a few miners' cabins, a shop or two, the engine and shaft houses. The embryo town was built among the charred stumps without order, on dry ground if possible, among drift boulders or knobs of trap. It often happened that the lode to be worked passed under a cedar swamp, wet and tangled. This added to the difficulty of the situation as well as the gloom of the place, for the swamp had to be drained and filled up with rock and other debris to make a foundation for the mine buildings. Some of the finest and largest towns in the upper peninsula were built in cedar swamps upon piles of rock filling.

JOHN H. FOSTER, *Life in the Copper Mines of Lake Superior,* 1924.

THE PICTURED ROCKS may be described, in general terms, as a series of sandstone bluffs extending along the shore of Lake Superior for about five miles and rising, in most places, vertically from the water, without any beach at the base, to a height varying from fifty to nearly two hundred feet. Were they simply a line of cliffs, they might not, so far as relates to height or extent, be worthy of rank among great natural curiosities, although such an assemblage of rocky strata, washed by the waves of the Great Lakes, would not, under any circumstances, be destitute of grandeur. To the voyager, coasting along their base in a frail canoe they would, at all times, be an object of dread; the recoil of the surf, the rockbound coast affording for miles no place of refuge; the lowering sky, the rising wind — all these would excite his apprehension, and induce him to apply vigorous oar until the dreaded wall was past.

MICHIGAN PIONEER AND HISTORICAL COLLECTIONS, 1924.

THE IMMENSE STRETCH OF COAST that we had just passed does not present a single noteworthy view. It is a plain covered with forests. The ensemble however, produces a profound and durable impression. This lake without sails, this shore which does not yet show any trace of the passage of man, this eternal forest which borders it; all that, I assure you is not grand in poetry only; it's the most extraordinary spectacle that I have seen in my life.

ALEXIS DE TOCQUEVILLE, from his journal, 1831.

ACROSS HER T-SHIRT was ski. She leafed through *Stalking the Wild Asparagus* in the college bookstore. I was in the middle of Michigan and looking for a place to go next, so I asked whether she lived in Mt. Pleasant, but she didn't look up. I tapped her arm.

"I'm from Missouri. Traveling. I'd like to find a good place to visit in Michigan." She watched but said nothing. "Maybe you know a nice spot." She just stared. Northerners really carry taciturnity too far, I thought.

A clerk came up and said, "She's deaf. Probably having trouble reading your lips." He repeated what I'd asked.

She said, "Oh," and put the book down. Holding up her right hand as if to say "How" in Hollywood Indian fashion, she said, "Dumb."

"Dumb?" the clerk repeated. I didn't know whether she meant me or herself.

"Dumb Miss Ginn," she said, and wagged her right thumb.

"Thumb of Michigan?" the clerk asked.

The girl smiled, wagged her thumb again, and nodded. "Berry Bootful."

"It's very beautiful," the clerk translated.

Looking at her ski T-shirt, I said, "Do you ski on the Thumb?"

"Dumbs to plat. By dames car water ski."

"Thumb's too flat to ski," the clerk said. "Her name's Karworski."

So that was how I ended up on the Thumb of Michigan.

WILLIAM LEAST HEAT MOON, *Blue Highways: A Journey into America*, 1982.

THE EARLY HISTORY of that part of our state is full of names of distinguished explorers and geographers. Such men as LaSalle, Marquette, Mesnard, Bayfield, Henry R. Schoolcraft, Cass and Houghton present an imposing array of adventurous spirits. But of their hardy followers, of the humble men of the rank and file, of individual independent pioneer explorers, we do not hear so much. Yet they were important factors in all organized expeditions; as voyageurs, hunters and packers, they were an indispensable element of success. And the independent explorer and settler, who ventured into the forest alone, unaided by capital or advantageous circumstances, all deserve some recognition. Common men, without the aid of whose brawn or sinew, sturdy bravery and enduring patience, the world would be much poorer, if not bankrupt in time, find few to sing their praises, and they are generally too modest to become their own chroniclers.

JOHN H. FOSTER, *Some Incidents of Pioneer Life in the Upper Peninsula of Michigan*, 1924.

I AM IN A COUNTRY where all is life and animation, where I hear on every side the sound of exultation, where everyone speaks of the past with triumph, the present with delight, the future with growing confidence and anticipation. Is not this a community in which one may rejoice to live? Is not this a land in which one may be proud to be received as a citizen? Is not this a land in which one may be happy to fix his destiny and ambition? I answer for one. Am I asked how long I mean to remain here. I answer as long as I live.

ANONYMOUS MICHIGAN FARMER, ca. 1830.

HORTONS BAY, the town, was only five houses on the main road between Boyne City and Charlevoix. There was the general store and post office with a high false front and maybe a wagon hitched out in front. Smith's house, Stroud's house, Dillworth's house, Horton's house and Vanhoosen's house. The houses were in a big grove of elm trees and the road was very sandy. There was farming country and timber each way up the road. Up the road a ways was the Methodist church and down the road the other direction was the township school. A blacksmith shop was painted red and faced the school.

A steep sandy road ran down the hill to the bay through the timber. From Smith's back door you could look out across the woods that ran down to the lake and across the bay. It was very beautiful in the spring and summer, the bay blue and bright and usually whitecaps on the lake out beyond the point from the breeze blowing from Charlevoix and Lake Michigan. From Smith's back door Liz could see ore barges way out in the lake going toward Boyne City. When she looked at them they didn't seem to be moving at all but if she went in and dried some more dishes and then came out again they would be out of sight beyond the point.

ERNEST HEMINGWAY, *Up in Michigan*, 1921.

HAZY SKYLINES. Chemical red sunsets. A yeasty gritty taste to the air — how easy to become addicted! And elsewhere, whatever constitutes elsewhere, will never quite satisfy. Much motion — Brownian, ceaseless — mesmerizing — a landscape of grids interrupted by sharp-slanted drives, freeways snaking through neighborhoods, cutting streets in two. A city of streets. Freeways. Overpasses, railroad tracks, razed buildings and weedy vacant lots and billboards and houses, houses, blocks and acres and galaxies of houses, stretching out forever. I shut my eyes and suddenly I am there again driving south along Livernois in the rain, meaning to get on the John Lodge just above Fenkell. Or am I driving on Six Mile Road east to Woodward. Or making the turn off Eight Mile and Litchfield, grateful to be home... Those streets. Those years. Livernois. Gratoit. Grand River. John R. Outer Drive. Michigan. Cass. 2nd. 3rd. Woodward. Jefferson. Vernor. Fort. Jos. Campau. Dequindre. Warren. Hancock. Beaubien. Brush. Freud. Randolph. Ceaseless motion, the pulse of the city. The beat. The beat. A place of romance, the quintessential American city.

JOYCE CAROL OATES, "Visions of Detroit," 1986.

MICHIGAN WILL BECOME A STATE; it is now an important area; since the spring of 1831 we have had every day a steamboat from Buffalo and one leaving Detroit. There are often two or three hundred passengers who come to settle in Michigan. Many thousand dollars were appropriated this year by Congress to begin or to lengthen five different roads or turnpikes in various directions of which two stretch from Detroit to (Lake) Michigan. You can judge for yourself; the Americans are asking me for a college wherein French will be one of the principal studies and offer to help me with the buildings. Success is beyond a doubt.

FATHER GABRIEL RICHARD, letter to Bossuet Richard, 1832.

MISSILIMACKINAC IS AN ISLAND famous in these regions, is more than a league in diameter and elevated in some places by such high cliffs as to be seen more than twelve leagues off. It is situated in the strait forming the communication between Lakes Huron and Illinois (Michigan). It is the key and as it were, the gateway for all the tribes from the south, as the Sault is for those of the north, there being in this section of the country only two passages by water, for a great number of nations have to go by one or the other to reach the French settlements.

FATHER JACQUES MARQUETTE, letter, 1671.

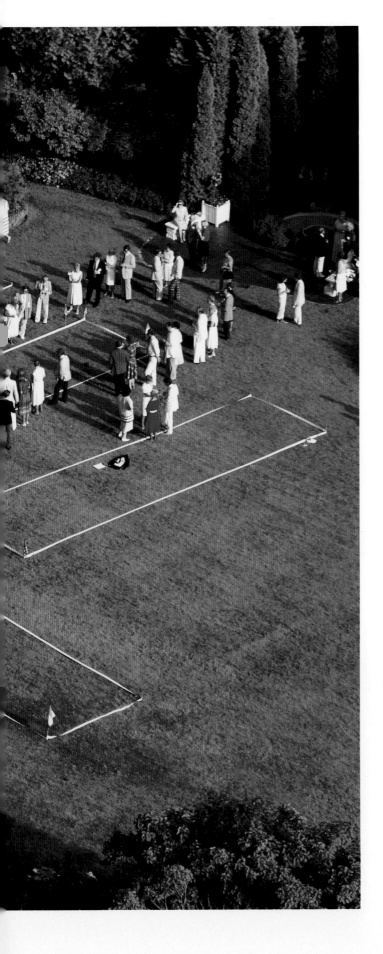

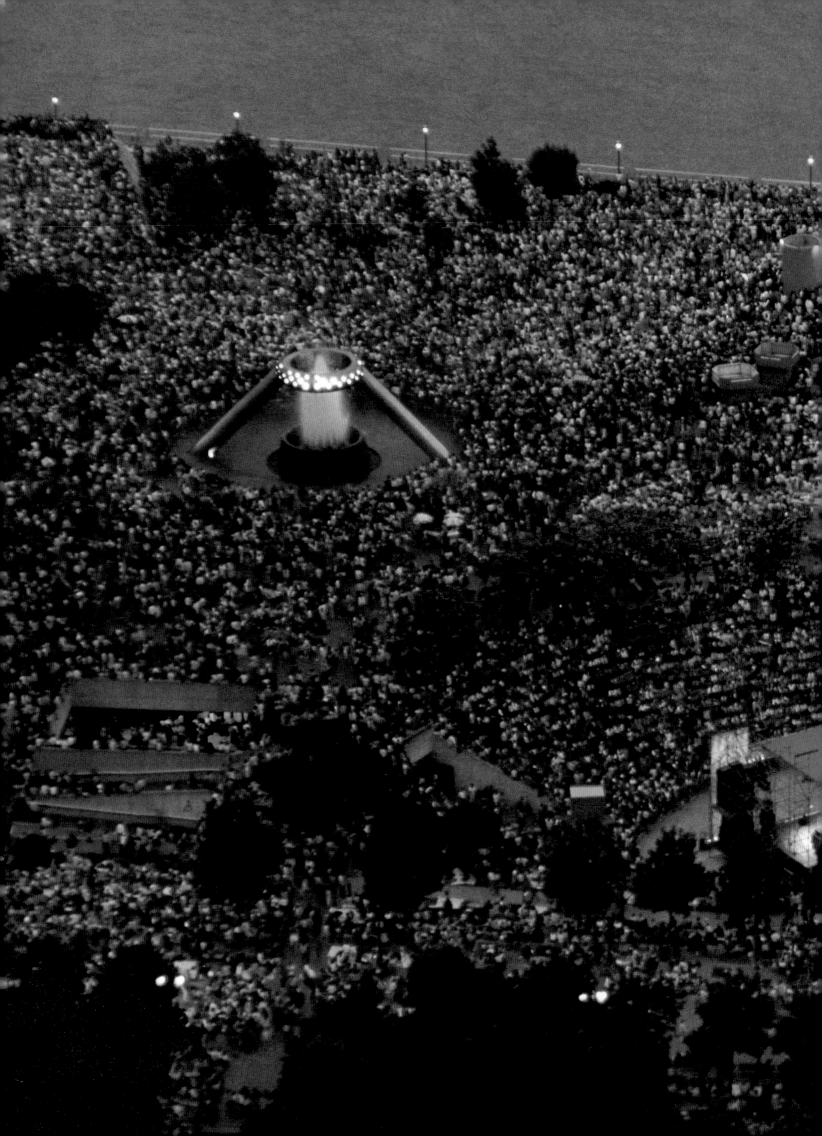

NOTES

2-3
DEADMAN'S VALLEY, MANCELONA. The valley received its name after a lumberjack was killed in a logging accident here.

4-5
FARM, SOUTH LYON. Long recognized as a manufacturing power, Michigan is a leader in agriculture as well. Michigan farmers produce 96 percent of the nation's navy beans and 75 percent of the country's cherry crop.

6-7
WEST SIDE, DETROIT, FROM ROOF OF PENOBSCOT BUILDING. The name of Detroit, founded in 1701, comes from the French phrase "le place du detroit," which means "the place of the strait." Detroit was an important outpost in French attempts to control the fur trade in the New World. It became a British outpost after the French-Indian War. In 1796 when General "Mad" Anthony Wayne defeated the British in the Battle of Fallen Timbers, Detroit became an American city for the first time.

8
ANTIQUE CAR SHOW, MEADOWBROOK HALL, ROCHESTER. Meadowbrook Hall was once the home of lumber baron Alfred G. Wilson. Many men who made their fortunes in the lumber industry later became investors in Detroit's fledgling automobile industry at the turn of the century.

10
GRAND HOTEL, MACKINAC ISLAND.

12
FARMHOUSE, NEAR MONROE.

14
WINTER SCENE ALONG M-72, NEAR GRAYLING.

15
BARN PAINTING.

16
INDIAN BURIAL GROUND, L'ANSE. Michigan was the home of several tribes of Indians in the 17th and 18th centuries. The principal tribes were the Chippewa-Ojibwa, Ottawa, and Potawatomis. Today Michigan has four reservations: L'Anse, Hannahville, Bay Mills in the Upper Peninsula, and Isabella near Mt. Pleasant.

17
WHITE PINE TREES. The white pine is the official state tree of Michigan. White pines have been used extensively in reforestation efforts due to their hardiness and the excellent shade they provide.

18-19
FORT MICHILIMACKINAC, MACKINAW CITY. Michilimackinac State Park houses an authentic restoration of the original French fort built in 1715. During Pontiac's rebellion, the fort was the scene of a bloody massacre. Loinclothed Indians loyal to Pontiac started a lacrosse game outside the fort walls. The game soon attracted the attention of the soldiers in the fort, as the Indians had hoped. At a pre-arranged signal, the Indians threw the lacrosse ball over the

wall. When the soldiers opened the gates to allow the game to continue, the Indians rushed in. The braves took weapons which the Indian women had concealed under their robes and blankets and massacred the soldiers in the fort.

20
SLEEPING BEAR DUNES NATIONAL LAKESHORE, NEAR EMPIRE. In 1970 Congress designated 34 miles of Lake Michigan shoreline as the Sleeping Bear Dunes National Lakeshore. A Chippewa legend tells of a mother bear that tried to swim across Lake Michigan from Wisconsin with her two cubs. Nearing shore, the exhausted cubs fell behind. The mother bear climbed to the top of a bluff to watch for her offspring. They never reached her, and today she can be seen as the Sleeping Bear, a solitary dune covered with dark trees and shrubs. Her cubs are the Manitou Islands which lie a few miles offshore.

21
STREAM IN COPPER HARBOR AREA, NEAR HOUGHTON. Most historians agree that Etienne Brule is likely to have been the first white man to discover Michigan, spending the winter of 1618-19 near Sault Ste. Marie. On a later trip up the St. Mary's River into Lake Superior, Brule returned with nuggets and a description of the Upper Peninsula. When other explorers entered Copper Harbor, they found nuggets so pure that they needed only to be hammered into shape. However, the copper deposits in the area proved unfruitful. Today the area is one of the most beautiful resort areas in the state.

22-23
IRON-WORKERS DORMITORY AND IRON SMELTER, FA-YETTE STATE PARK. The Jackson Iron Company purchased the Fayette site in 1864. It was chosen because the area contained limestone and a great quantity of hardwood trees that could be used to make charcoal for the smelting process. By 1869 Fayette had become a "boom town" with a store, office building, hotel, post office, and even an opera house. It soon became cheaper to smelt ore at the furnaces on Lake Erie, however, and Fayette, like other Michigan mining towns, faded into obscurity. It survives today as a state park.

24-25
SUSPENSION BRIDGE, HOUGHTON AND HANCOCK. Houghton is named for Dr. Douglas Houghton, a Detroit physician and scientist who visited the area in 1831-32 with Henry School-craft. He later contracted with the federal government to conduct official geological surveys here. Those surveys are generally credited with fostering the mining boom that later swept the area. The copper-bearing geological formations found here are believed to be the oldest rock formations in the world.

27
LIGHTHOUSE, EAGLE HARBOR. Lake Superior, the world's largest inland lake, has taken its toll of ships and lives. In 1975, sea-sized waves and screaming winds sent the *Edmund Fitzgerald*, a 729-foot ore-carrying freighter, to its watery depths. All 29 crewmen aboard were lost.

28-29
SOO LOCKS, SAULT STE. MARIE. Where Lake Superior joins Lake Huron, the water level drops 21 feet in less than a mile. Taking advantage of this natural phenomenon, the Soo Locks were first constructed in the 19th century. During World War II, the locks, referred to as the "jugular vein of North America," were considered so important strategically that 20,000 troops were stationed here to protect them. With modern improvements, the locks now are capable of moving four ocean-going freighters simultaneously. The lock system and the opening of the St. Lawrence Seaway have made Michigan America's "fourth seacoast."

30
SKI RESORT, LEELANAU.

31
SLEEPING BEAR DUNES NATIONAL LAKESHORE.

32
PINE STUMPS, STANDISH. A few stumps are all that is left of Michigan's 19th-century lumber industry. Today much of the state has been reforested, and the great pine trees have made a remarkable comeback.

33
RED SUMAC AND WHITE PINE.

34
U.S. HIGHWAY 41, NEAR COPPER HARBOR. The earliest roads in Michigan were constructed of wooden planks. They worked well until shifting and freezing of the ground forced the boards out of alignment, creating a washboard effect. Riding in a stagecoach on a plank road from Kalamazoo to Grand Rapids, Mark Twain remarked that the ride would have been enjoyable had not "some unconscionable scoundrel now and then dropped a plank across the road."

35
LAKE MACATAWA, NEAR HOLLAND. Michigan is considered the boating capital of the world. There are more registered boats per capita in Michigan than in any other state.

36
TURKEY FARM, NEAR MANCELONA.

37
FARM, CLARE.

38-39
FARMS, GRAND TRAVERSE BAY AREA.

40
CHATEAU GRAND TRAVERSE VINEYARDS, MISSION PENINSULA.

41
PUMPKIN FARM, ANN ARBOR.

42
CHERRY ORCHARD, TRAVERSE CITY. A half-acre cherry orchard planted near Traverse City in the 1880s has multiplied into an industry that produces 78 million pounds of cherries a year.

43
FARMER, NEAR TEMPERANCE.

44
HOT-AIR BALLOON, BATTLE CREEK. Battle Creek, which takes its name from a "battle" that occurred here between an Indian and a land surveyor in 1825, has earned its fame by filling the nation's cereal bowl. W.K. Kellogg and C.W. Post founded the cereal business here; their plants are the largest of their type anywhere. Battle Creek is also the grave site of Sojourner Truth, the famous anti-slavery crusader.

45

MAIN STREET, HOMER. Typical of many small Michigan towns, Homer was settled on the banks of a river. Milton Barney was Homer's first permanent settler, building a grist mill here on the Kalamazoo River in 1832.

46

STREET SCENE, IONIA. Construction began on the Ionia County Courthouse in 1883 and ended in 1886. This Renaissance-revival structure is largely composed of pink Ionia sandstone.

47

COLONIAL DAYS, GREENFIELD VILLAGE AND THE HENRY FORD MUSEUM. The Greenfield Village-Henry Ford Museum is an indoor-outdoor museum complex that draws over one million visitors each year. The complex was built by Henry Ford as a tribute to the culture, resourcefulness, and technology of the U.S. and was dedicated to Thomas Edison in 1929. The museum occupies 12 acres and includes major collections in transportation, power and machinery, and agriculture. Greenfield Village comprises more than 80 buildings from the 17th, 18th, and 19th centuries which were moved here from all parts of the country. Among them are Henry Ford's birthplace, Edison's Menlo Park laboratory, and the home of Luther Burbank.

48

DOOR DETAIL, TRAVERSE CITY HOME.

49

STREET SCENE, MONROE. Monroe is the birthplace of General George Armstrong Custer. Artifacts from his life are on display at the Monroe County Historical Museum.

50

SHIAWASSEE COUNTY COURTHOUSE, CORUNNA. Built in 1904-05, the Shiawassee County Courthouse is patterned in the Renaissance-revival style. The courthouse has a multi-tiered central tower with Corinthian columns on the portico. Nominated to the National Register of Historic Places, the courthouse occupies two city blocks in Corunna's central business district.

51

LIVINGSTON COUNTY COURTHOUSE, HOWELL.

52-53

STATE CAPITOL, LANSING. When the capital of Michigan was located here in 1847, the city consisted of one log house and a sawmill. Today, Lansing is not only the seat of the state government, but also the headquarters for many trade and professional groups. The capitol building was completed in 1878 and features a hand-worked tin dome, imported English etched-glass windows, and original iron chandeliers by Tiffany's of New York.

54

CENTRAL REFORMED CHURCH, GRAND RAPIDS. Grand Rapids, Kalamazoo, and Holland are the three points of Michigan's "Dutch triangle." The first wave of Dutch immigrants came in the mid-19th century to escape poverty as well as state interference in the Reformed Church of the Netherlands. Unemployment and overcrowding in Holland brought a second major wave of immigration after World War II.

55

OUTDOOR CONCERT, FLINT. Flint is Michigan's third-largest city and was the birthplace of General Motors Corporation. A center for the manufacture of wagons and carriages in the 19th century, the city was well prepared for the advent of the automobile industry.

56

HOUSE, EAGLE RIVER. The stark, utilitarian styling of homes built in the Upper Peninsula during the Victorian era contrasts greatly with the ornate style of other homes built in that period. Immigrants working in the mines and lumber camps chose simple construction for their homes that was well suited for life on Michigan's frontier.

57

HONOLULU HOUSE, MARSHALL. This home was built in 1860 by the former U.S. consul to the Hawaiian Islands. The structure contains many period furnishings and artifacts and serves as headquarters for the Marshall Historical Society.

58

OAK HILL INTERIOR, MARSHALL.

59

WEST BLUFF HOME, MACKINAC ISLAND. This Lincrusta Walton covering was a popular wall-covering in the Victorian era. It was developed by the makers of linoleum.

60-61

DOW GARDENS, MIDLAND. The gardens of the home of Herbert H. Dow of the Dow Chemical Company cover 66 acres and provide a popular tourist site for visitors to Midland.

62

MEYER MAY HOME, GRAND RAPIDS.

63

MELWYN SMITH HOUSE, BLOOMFIELD HILLS. The Meyer May and Melwyn Smith homes are two of the 33 buildings in Michigan designed by Frank Lloyd Wright, considered America's greatest native-born architect.

64-65

WATER STREET PAVILION, FLINT.

66
HERMAN MILLER FURNITURE FACTORY, ZEELAND. The enormous lumber industry in Michigan in the 19th century turned the Grand Rapids area into a world-renowned furniture-producing center.

67
"LA GRANDE VITESSE," GRAND RAPIDS. Situated in front of the county building, the 42-ton sculpture by Alexander Calder is Grand Rapids' most popular landmark. The city was settled in 1826 when Louis Campau established an Indian trading post. It derives its name from the rapids of the Grand River, which flows through the heart of the city.

68-69
RAILROADS, FLINT. The first railroad line to operate in Michigan ran between Detroit and Birmingham in 1838. The first cars were pulled by horses. In 1839, a steam locomotive was added.

70-71
FORD MOTOR COMPANY PLANT, RIVER ROUGE. The River Rouge factory, designed by Albert Kahn, is considered to be the most complete auto-making facility in the world. It occupies 1,100 acres and at one time employed over 100,000 workers. Regarded as one of the greatest industrial architects of all time, Kahn designed over 1,000 buildings for the Ford Motor Company as well as hundreds of others for General Motors and Chrysler.

72
WATER TOWER, GENERAL MOTORS TECHNICAL CENTER, WARREN.

73
ENGINE BLOCKS, DETROIT DIESEL, ROMULUS.

74
GRAVEL PIT, LUDINGTON. Ludington was originally named Père Marquette in honor of the missionary-explorer who died here in 1675. The town was later renamed in honor of James Ludington, a 19th-century lumber baron. Ludington is a busy port city, offering a car-ferry service between Michigan and Wisconsin.

75
DETROIT RIVER.

76-77
FREIGHTER, ROUGE RIVER. While shipping is important to the state, only 120 of the 58,160 river miles in Michigan are classified as "major waterway," and no Michigan river is designated as a "principal river" of the U.S., since their waters drain into the Great Lakes before sufficient volume is generated for the principal-river designation.

78
DETROIT SKYLINE. Dominating Detroit's skyline is the 71-story Renaissance Center, which houses the world's tallest hotel and provides space for more than 10,000 office workers.

80-81
TIGER STADIUM, DETROIT. With more than 52,000 seats, Tiger Stadium took its present shape in the 1930s.

82
BOBLO ISLAND, DETROIT. This popular 272-acre amusement park is located on Boblo Island in the Detroit River. The park contains numerous rides and attractions and is accessible only by boat.

83
LABOR DAY PARADE, DETROIT.

84
UNIVERSITY OF MICHIGAN, ANN ARBOR. Founded in Detroit in 1817, the university was moved to Ann Arbor in 1837. It is one of the largest universities in the country, with an enrollment of over 35,000 students.

85
DANCER, CRANBROOK ACADEMY OF ART, BLOOMFIELD HILLS. Cranbrook is located on the former estate of newspaper publisher George G. Boothe. The estate contains four separate educational institutions, each important to the cultural life of Michigan.

86-87
CRANBROOK ACADEMY OF ART.

88-89
MACKINAC ISLAND. Mackinac Island was called the "great turtle" by the Indians, who believed its towering heights were shaped by supernatural forces. It came into permanent U.S. possession after the War of 1812.

90
MACKINAC ISLAND. Site of the Grand Hotel, Mackinac Island has been a resort area since the decline of the fur trade more than a century ago. Southern planters vacationed here with their families before the Civil War; wealthy Chicagoans took their place in the years following the war. Today the island retains the ambience of the 19th century. No automobiles are allowed; transportation is by horse or bicycle only.

91
VERANDA, GRAND HOTEL.

92
LAWN BOWLING, MACKINAC ISLAND.

93
BICYCLISTS, MACKINAC ISLAND.

94-95
MACKINAC BRIDGE. This imposing structure has reduced crossing time over the Straits of Mackinac to just ten minutes by car. The 8,344-foot distance between cable-anchors makes Mackinac the world's longest suspension bridge.

96-97
INTERNATIONAL FREEDOM FESTIVAL, HART PLAZA, DETROIT.

98-99
PUMPKIN FARM, ANN ARBOR.

100
HEMLOCKS, PORCUPINE MOUNTAINS STATE PARK.

102
ANNUNCIATION. A painting of the annunciation in a garden along Lake Michigan's shore stands in vivid contrast to the formal "La Grande Vitesse" sculpture in Grand Rapids. Art can be found everywhere along the back roads of Michigan.

104
MACKINAC BRIDGE, MACKINAW CITY.

Ernest Hemingway, excerpted from "Up in Michigan" from THE SHORT STORIES OF ERNEST HEMINGWAY. Copyright 1938 Ernest Hemingway; copyright renewed ©1966 Mary Hemingway. Reprinted with the permission of Charles Scribner's Sons. Excerpt from ANATOMY OF A MURDER by Robert Traver, copyright 1958, St. Martin's Press, Inc. Reprinted by permission of the publisher. Excerpt from MICHIGAN: A BICENTENNIAL HISTORY by Bruce Catton, copyright ©1984, W. W. Norton & Company, Inc. Reprinted by permission of the publisher. Excerpt from BLUE HIGHWAYS: A JOURNEY INTO AMERICA by William Least Heat Moon. Copyright ©1982 by William Least Heat Moon. Reprinted by permission of Little, Brown and Company. Excerpt from "Visions of Detroit" by Joyce Carol Oates. Reprinted by permission of the MICHIGAN QUARTERLY REVIEW.

The publisher has made a thorough effort to locate all persons having any rights or interests in material, and to clear reprint permissions. If any required acknowledgments have been omitted or any rights overlooked, we regret the error.